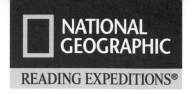
PLANET PROTECTORS

What's Poisoning the Garden?

By Barbara Keeler
Illustrated by Dan Brown

PICTURE CREDITS
3 (top left & right), 4 (top right), 5 (top left), 6 (top right), 7 (top left), 60 (top right), 61 (top left), 61 (top center), 62 (top right), 63 (top left), 64 (top left & right) Corbis; 4 (top left), 6 (top left), 60 (top left), 62 (top left) © Artville; 4 (bottom) © Dennis MacDonald/Alamy; 5 (top right), 7 (top right), 61 (top right), 63 (top right) Getty Images; 5 (top center) © Joel W. Rogers/Corbis; 60 © Holger Winkler/zefa/Corbis; 62 © Jeff Greenberg/Peter Arnold, Inc.; 64 © Kenneth Garrett/National Geographic Image Collection.

PUBLISHED BY THE NATIONAL GEOGRAPHIC SOCIETY
Produced through the worldwide resources of the National Geographic Society, John M. Fahey, Jr., President and Chief Executive Officer; Gilbert M. Grosvenor, Chairman of the Board.

PREPARED BY NATIONAL GEOGRAPHIC SCHOOL PUBLISHING
Sheron Long, Chief Executive Officer; Samuel Gesumaria, President; Francis Downey, Vice President and Publisher; Richard Easby, Editorial Manager; Anne M. Stone, Editor; Margaret Sidlosky, Director of Design and Illustrations; Jim Hiscott, Design Manager; Cynthia Olson, Ruth Ann Thompson, Art Directors; Matt Wascavage, Director of Publishing Services; Lisa Pergolizzi, Production Manager.

MANUFACTURING AND QUALITY CONTROL
Christopher A. Liedel, Chief Financial Officer; Phillip L. Schlosser, Vice President; Clifton M. Brown III, Director.

CONSULTANT
Mary Anne Wengel

BOOK DESIGN
Steve Curtis Design, Inc.

Published by the National Geographic Society
1145 17th Street N.W.
Washington, D.C. 20036-4688

Product #4U1005112
ISBN: 978-1-4263-5105-1

Printed in Mexico.

12
10 9 8 7 6 5 4 3 2

TABLE OF CONTENTS

What Are Pesticides?

When people think of pesticides they often think of bugs. Bug spray can be used to kill roaches or ants. These pesticides are called insecticides. But "pests" can also be weeds. Pesticides that kill pesky plants are called herbicides. Other pesticides fight plant disease. Rodenticides kill rats and other rodents.

Pesticides are toxic to living things. Toxic means poisonous. Some pesticides are harmful to humans. Others are less harmful. Sometimes people who are exposed to pesticides get sick. They can have rashes, burns, or damage to their organs. Pesticides have to be handled and used very carefully.

The sign reads:

COMPOSTABLES ONLY

NO — MORNING GLORY
COMFREY ROOTS
QUACK GRASS
PLACE THESE THINGS IN THE
ADJACENT SHORT BINS

PLEASE — NO PLASTIC OR
STRING IN THESE
BINS

What Is Composting?

Composting is a way of recycling grass clippings, fallen leaves, and some food scraps. These waste items decompose or break down until they are compost. Compost is similar to soil and great for growing plants.

All dead plants decompose in nature. However, our backyards produce a lot of waste. This waste includes grass clippings during the summer and leaves in the fall. Many people put this waste in the trash. Many communities do something different. They collect all the yard waste and take it to a giant compost pile. The compost pile is designed so that yard waste decomposes quickly. Once the yard waste has decomposed it forms compost. People use the compost in their gardens.

Meet the Characters

Holly

Holly is in the sixth grade. She likes her best friend, Kizzy, but she wonders what it would be like to be in a cool crowd. Meanwhile, other problems are popping up for Holly. She has to help solve a mystery at her school.

Skip

Skip is Holly's older brother. He is in the eighth grade. He is well liked in school and looks after Holly.

April

April Brown decides who is in the cool club of the sixth grade. Many girls want to be her friend. She can be mean, and girls are afraid of her.

Mr. Stone

Mr. Stone is a science teacher and Kizzy's dad. He has set up an organic garden at the school. The students love to work in the garden.

Kizzy

Kizzy is Holly's best friend. She is loyal and is hurt because Holly is not as loyal to her. Her father is the school's science teacher.

CHAPTER 1

Missing Fish

— AUGUST 2001 —

A fishing line whipped through the air behind Holly. Skip's baited hook splashed into the water about ten feet from Holly's. It sent ripples through the still pool.

Holly was fishing with her brother, Skip, and his friend Jeff. After an hour without a bite, Holly asked, "Remember how many fish we used to catch?"

"How long have we been here anyway?" asked Jeff. "Nobody's had a nibble."

"Maybe it's just as well," said Skip. "Mr. Stone says that pesticides from farms are stored in fish tissues."

"Gross!" said Holly. "Maybe we shouldn't eat them."

"Pesticides includes insecticides to kill insects, herbicides to kill weeds, and others to kill disease. Which kind are stored?" asked Jeff.

"All of them," said Skip. "Most of the pesticides in the creeks and rivers come from the farms around here. Mr. Stone says corn farms use the most insecticides. Almost all farmers used herbicides to kill weeds."

"At least we can still find frogs here," said Holly. I haven't seen any frogs near our house for a long time."

"In seventh grade we learned that a drop in the number of frogs may be a sign of pollution," said Jeff.

"We haven't caught any fish near our house for a year," said Skip. "I thought if we hiked up higher than the farms, the pesticides wouldn't be in the water."

"Kizzy says some of the fish swim upstream to breed," explained Holly. "She also says some swim upstream after they hatch. So something that kills fish downstream can affect the number of fish upstream too."

"How did she learn all that?" asked Skip.

"Hello?! Her father is our science teacher," said Holly.

They were silent for a while, looking at the rippling water. Holly looked at the red, green, and yellow leaves on the trees that hugged the banks of the creek. They shut out most of the sunlight. Tiny slivers of light slipped between the leaves and danced on the water.

Holly looked at Skip. "Dad made you take me with you, didn't he?"

Skip dropped his eyes to his fishing line. "I don't mind. Dad felt sorry for you because you had nobody to hang out with today. I thought April Brown was coming over."

"She canceled at the last minute," said Holly.

Skip and Jeff exchanged looks. "Did you tell her Jeff and I were going fishing?" asked Ben.

"Yes, I told her we'd have the TV to ourselves."

"How long after that did she cancel?" asked Jeff.

"She called back five minutes later. Why?"

"No reason," said Jeff.

"Why didn't you hang out with Kizzy?" asked Skip. "You guys have been best friends since second grade."

"She's gone to the city with Grace's family," said Holly. "They didn't invite me."

"I can't blame Kizzy," said Skip, "the way you've been dumping her every time April gives you a call."

"I don't understand that," said Jeff. "I've never seen April do anything except gossip and giggle. She's no fun to be around. Kizzy is interesting to talk to. In fact I wish she were here today. She tells us all the science behind fishing. She has a great sense of humor, too."

"April's thinking of letting me join the AAA Club."

"You mean April's Amazing Airheads?" asked Skip.

"It's secret what the letters stand for," said April. "Only club members know."

"We just call them the Queen Bees," said Jeff. "Why would you blow off a great friend like Kizzy for them? I don't understand you."

"I've never had a chance to hang out with a cool crowd before," said Holly. "You don't know what that's like. In your grade, you're the big wheels everyone wants to hang out with."

"There's a difference though," said Jeff. "Sis says its not so much that everyone likes April." Jeff's sister was in the fifth grade. "She gives all the good parties, and she is supposed to be fun. But it's more that the girls are afraid of her. She and her crowd are such gossips. They can ruin a reputation. So the girls all play up to them."

Skip changed the subject. "How come you didn't hang out with Will? You've been friends since you were babies."

"He's doing stuff with the guys today." Holly thought sadly about how things changed after a certain age. At 11, it was harder for girls and boys to hang out the way they did when they were younger.

After another hour of fishing with no luck, they packed their gear. Holly looked at the clear, rushing water. She wondered if pesticides were really killing the fish.

As they stepped out of the thicket of trees and bushes, the moist, cool air gave way to hot, dry air. Gone was the heavy smell of wet earth and leaves. In its place was the scent of dry grass and pine trees.

They hiked home over the grass covered hills. The sun beat down on their shoulders. Holly took every chance to pass under the shade of a pine tree.

Just before they reached town, the trail turned into a paved path. The path ran between the golf course and the creek. Skip said, "I bet Mr. Brown uses tons of herbicides to kill the weeds on his golf course. Probably insecticides, too, to kill the bugs. Look, they probably run off into the creek with every rain."

"I don't see many people playing golf," said Holly.

"What were the Browns thinking, opening a golf course here? On nice days the people here would rather hike, fish, or play other sports," said Skip.

"Or work in their gardens," said Holly. "Mrs. Brown spends a lot of time in hers. She has the most beautiful roses in town."

"She always brags about her green, weed-free lawn," said Jeff. "I bet she uses enough weed killer and bug killer to kill all the fish in the creek."

Holly's street dead-ended at the creek near the golf course. As they walked along the sidewalk, Holly admired the lawns on her block. Dotted here and there with dandelions and clover, they were much prettier than the solid green lawns that were treated with herbicides. Holly and Kizzy's parents had persuaded most of their neighbors to stop using herbicides.

Most of the neighbors also grew vegetables and fruit. They grew them without using any kind of pesticide.

Some neighbors got their exercise pulling weeds from the lawn and garden. Others hired Holly, Kizzy, and Will to pull weeds.

Kizzy's mother, Dr. Stone, had shown the neighbors how to make tea from clover, dandelions, and other weed plants. She also taught them delicious ways to cook young dandelion greens.

Dr. Stone was an **acupuncturist.** Since she had been treating Holly, her asthma attacks had stopped.

At home, Holly picked up the town newspaper and leafed through it. A local doctor had written an article in the health section.

"Listen to this, Skip," she said. "Dr. Gray, from the hospital says scientists have found higher levels of cancer in people who live near farms where pesticides are used."

"I already knew that," said Skip.

"Yes, but listen," said Holly, "He says the rate of cancer in our town is very high. Nobody can prove the cancer is caused by pesticides, but Dr. Gray thinks it is."

"What does he think we should do?"

"He says everyone should buy fruits and vegetables that are organic or grown without pesticides. They should

---

acupuncturist – a medical person who pricks parts of the body with fine needles to relieve pain or cure disease

demand organic products from their stores. That will encourage farmers to grow crops without pesticides. Most important, people should stop using pesticides in their yards, he says."

"Some of us are way ahead of him," said Skip. He was right. Many people in town were already trying to cut pesticide use. They were also worried about the effects of pesticides used on surrounding farms. Pesticides were used mostly on fields of corn and wheat.

"I know. That's why we started the organic garden at school," said Holly.

The students, parents, and teachers had been concerned about the effects of pesticides. They had worked together to get rid of all pesticides used on the school grounds. Instead of using weed killers, classes took turns pulling weeds. The science classes were studying ways of managing insect pests without poisons.

Some of the students had suggested starting a school organic garden. They wanted to prove that organic gardening could be successful, then maybe local farmers would cut their use of pesticides. Even better, they could give the vegetables they grew to a soup kitchen that fed hungry people.

They made sure to plant corn. More pesticides are used on corn than on most crops. The students wanted to show that corn could be grown without pesticides.

CHAPTER 2

The Mystery in the Garden

— AUGUST 2001 —

Holly looked forward to working in the school garden the next day. Kizzy, Holly, Skip, and many other students had volunteered to keep the garden going during the summer. They picked the vegetables and gave them to the soup kitchen.

The next morning, Holly, Kizzy, and Skip walked to the school. The sun hung low in the sky. Its rays slanted through the morning mist. The kids cast long shadows as they walked along. As they reached the school garden, some blossoms were just beginning to open in the morning sun. Local farmers were invited to visit the garden. The students took turns as tour guides. Today Holly, Kizzy, and Skip gave the tour. Ms. Lopez, the English teacher, supervised, but the students did all the talking.

Holly explained to the farmers, "We plant different crops in one area. When insects find a large area with one kind of crop they like, they hang around and breed."

"Good thinking," said one farmer. "A few years ago, I converted all of my land to cornfields. It was like painting a bull's-eye on my field. All the corn pests seem to find my fields now."

"After you have used pesticides for a while, the bugs and weeds are harder to control," said Kizzy. "It is a few of the stronger ones that are not killed. When they breed, the new bugs and weeds can also resist the pesticides. Over time, the population will become more and more **resistant** to the pesticides."

"Yes, the insects are already beginning to build up resistance. The weeds get resistant to weed killers too," said the farmer. "I find I have to use more pesticides each year to control bugs and weeds."

"There are other ways of controlling weeds. A neighbor of mine grazes his cows in his apple orchard," said another farmer. "The cows keeps the weeds down."

"I know the farmer you mean," said Holly. "My parents buy all of our milk, yoghurt, and apples from him. The apples are organic, and the cows eat only pesticide-free grass."

"I think I'm going to try grazing cows in my cherry orchard," said the farmer.

Then Kizzy explained the borders of marigolds and garlic. "These plants smell bad to some bugs. They drive them away."

"We also rotate crops instead of planting the same crop in the same place," said Skip. "This seems to break the life cycle of some bugs that breed in mostly one crop. Maybe it confuses them too."

----

resistant – not affected by something

"My father used to rotate crops," said one farmer. "It is better for the soil."

"We had to learn to do it right," said Skip. "Different crops need different nutrients. For example, spinach needs a lot of nitrogen. One year we plant spinach. The spinach takes nitrogen out of the soil. The next year we plant beans. Beans put nitrogen back into the soil."

"We even plant different kinds of beans, different kinds of tomatoes, and different kinds of peppers," said Kizzy. "That way if one kind can't resist a weather condition or a pest, another might survive."

One farmer was looking at a new plot of ground. They had dug it up and planted it a few weeks ago. "That garden doesn't look good," he said. "Can we take a look?"

Holly looked at Kizzy. They had noticed the new garden was not doing well. They couldn't say no, though.

In the garden, the farmers looked critically at the rows. They should be full of healthy plants. "What did you plant in this empty row?"

"Peas," said Holly.

"When?"

"A few weeks ago."

"That's plenty of time. They should be up by now."

Another farmer touched a bean plant in another row. "The leaves on these plants look strange. Notice how their leaves are cupped or rolled?"

"I've seen that in some weeds on my farm," said one farmer. "Sometimes they grow on the outer edge of a plot that's been sprayed with weed killer. The weed killer does that to their leaves, if it doesn't kill them."

"But we don't use weed killers," said Kizzy.

"Well, your other plots look great," said the corn farmer. "Your corn looks better than mine! You've given us something to think about." He and the other farmers said goodbye and walked toward their cars.

Holly watched them go. "I have Mom's cell phone. Let's call your dad."

About five minutes later, Mr. Stone, the science teacher and Kizzy's Dad, arrived. Kizzy showed him the empty rows and the strangely shaped leaves.

"That looks like herbicide damage all right," said Mr. Stone. "I don't know how to explain it, though."

"Our first two crops were great," said Holly. "Are we doing anything different?"

"All I can think of is that we planted different land this time," said Mr. Stone. "Turn this into a research project. I'll give you credit when you start sixth grade. See if you can figure out why plants in an organic garden might have herbicide damage."

Later Kizzy sat at the computer. Holly and Skip leaned over Kizzy's shoulder, watching the screen. Kizzy typed in the words *herbicide* and *organic* in the search field. Then she hit ENTER. Several entries came up. She opened one and read the first few paragraphs.

EARTH NEWS TODAY

HOME   NEWS   TECHNOLOGY   HEALTH   MESSAGE BOARD

Contaminated Composts Found in 3 States

LOS ANGELES – Traces of an herbicide have been found in compost in three states. The states are California, Washington, and Pennsylvania.

The herbicide, clopyralid, is toxic to garden vegetables. It is used mainly to kill weeds. Sadly, it can also kill vegetables such as peas, beans, peppers, tomatoes, and potatoes.

The lawn waste composting industry is worried about this discovery. Compost and recycling companies say that their businesses could go broke if herbicides are found in the compost.

Kizzy skimmed further down. She said "In Washington compost they've found enough herbicide to kill certain plants." She called to her Father, "Dad! I think we've found something!"

Mr. Stone came into the room and looked at the screen. He read quickly, and then looked up.

"Why don't you email Mark about this?" said Mr. Stone. Kizzy's older brother majored in **environmental science** at the state university. "He's studying the effects of farming methods on the environment."

"That's a good idea!" Kizzy typed in the message and then hit the send button. They all decided to go into the living room and wait for Mark's reply.

"We're having a problem only in the new plot," said Kizzy. "Why should it be different from the other plots?"

"I've got it!" said Holly. "We used all of our own compost from the school grounds on the first plots we farmed. We didn't have enough compost for the new plot, so we got some from the city compost pile."

"That's right!" said Skip. "We don't use any herbicides at school, so the yard waste in our compost wouldn't have any weed killers."

"Let's go see if Mark has replied," said Mr. Stone.

They all went back to Kizzy's room. Kizzy sat at the computer and clicked the icon for checking mail. A message popped up from Mark.

----

environmental science – the study of everything that surrounds a living thing

Email

New Mail   Reply   Forward

Dear Kizzy,

    Attached is an article from today's university newsletter. It says we have found herbicides in our compost too. Last year we found an herbicide called picloram. This year we found one called clopyralid. We tested the compost when we noticed that certain plants in our organic garden were not growing right.

    I know our town picks up yard waste and composts it. Too many people use herbicides, especially on their lawns. The kinds of herbicides we have found in our compost are not legal to use in backyards. They are used a lot in parks, on golf courses, and on other grassy areas, maybe in our town.

    When I come home, I'll take samples of your compost to test it.

    Skip was watching out the window. "Mom just drove up!" he said. Mom worked for the city Department of Waste Management. Her department was in charge of the city compost pile. "She should know about this."

    Everyone rushed next door and walked in with Mom. She dropped her briefcase and flopped down in her favorite chair. She began to rub her tired eyes. "What a day!" she said.

It's about to get worse," Mr. Stone said quietly.

Mom looked at the long faces. "What's wrong?"

"We think herbicides in the city compost are killing the plants in the school organic garden," said Holly.

"Yikes!" said Mom. "Herbicides are in our compost and the compost kills plants? Then how can we obey a law that says we have to compost yard waste?"

"What are you going to do?" asked Holly.

"I have to talk to city council about changing the law," said Mom. "But how should they change it? If we don't pick up lawn clippings, they go into the landfill. If we do, the weed killers poison the compost."

"We'll all help you think of something," said Holly. "Won't we, Mr. Stone?"

"Not tonight," said Mom. "I'm too tired. We have the rest of the summer. I'm not going to bring this up now. Half of the city council is on vacation."

The next day, April invited Holly to come over. She walked over with Consuela, who lived on her block. Consuela had been best friends with Grace. Then, at the end of last year, she started hanging out with April.

All the AAAs were at April's. It was a sunny day, and they were talking in the rose garden. April's parents were famous for their parties in the rose garden. So was April.

The latest songs blared from an outdoor speaker. A couple of girls had brought some gossip magazines.

Holly told the AAAs about the problems with the school garden. She was about to tell them about the compost, the herbicides, and the article she read. April interrupted. "Tell someone who cares. You hang around Kizzy too much."

April smirked. "And now Kizzy hangs out with Grace. What a loser Grace is. She always wears T-shirts with dumb slogans. 'Pesticides Poison the Planet'? Please!" All the girls sniggered, except Consuela and Holly.

For the rest of the day, they leafed through magazines and gossiped about movie stars, TV stars, and other girls. They also giggled and talked about which boys were the cutest. When April's favorite soap came on, they all took a break and watched it.

For the rest of the summer, Holly spent time with April whenever she could. She was not often invited to April's house. Usually, April wanted to come to Holly's.

When she wasn't with April, Holly hung out with Kizzy and Grace. Sometimes they worked in the school gardens or weeded their neighbors' yards. The rest of the time they hiked or shot hoops in Holly's back yard. It was much more fun than hanging out with the AAAs, but Holly was determined to be part of the in-crowd.

Holly also spent time with Will. He sometimes helped pull weeds in Holly's yard. Then they went to his house and pulled weeds. Sometimes they went fishing, but they didn't catch anything.

CHAPTER 3

The First Day of School

— SEPTEMBER 2001 —

The first day of school was bright and clear. The sun was shining, but a crispness in the air signaled that fall was on the way. Holly walked out the front door, and then headed back for a light jacket.

Holly walked with Kizzy, Grace, and Will. At the school grounds, they passed the new plot. A few plants with cupped leaves struggled for life.

As soon as they reached the playground, Will headed off to join the boys. The AAAs were standing near the door to home room when April called to Holly.

"Her Majesty summons," said Kizzy, looking at Holly.

"I'll—er—just see what she wants," said Holly.

"Right," said Kizzy.

When Holly drew near, April said, "I'm having a sleepover this weekend. I'd like you to come."

All through morning classes, Holly wondered if April would invite her to eat lunch with the AAAs. Last year, she had watched them at lunch, wondering what it was like to be part of the in-crowd. Maybe people would watch her this year.

When the lunch bell rang, Holly rushed into the hall. Lockers were clanging shut, and hundreds of feet shuffled toward the cafeteria.

At the door of the cafeteria, Holly saw Kizzy and Grace look up. On the other side of the cafeteria, April waved. Kizzy lowered her eyes as Holly walked over to join April and her crowd.

"Next period we're in the stupid garden," said April, taking out her salad. "I hate grubbing in the garden."

Holly didn't say anything. Gardening was her favorite activity of the week. She bit into her avocado sandwich with homegrown tomatoes and **clover** leaves.

Later, in the garden, Holly and Kizzy worked together picking beans and tomatoes. They had been partners since the first crop was planted. They both liked to sample the crisp beans fresh from the garden. When they moved to the tomato row, they breathed in the fragrance of the tomato plant leaves.

Gone was the crispness of the morning air, and the hot sun beat down. Beads of sweat trickled down their faces and necks. Their wet shirts clung to their backs.

-----

clover – a common plant that has leaves in groups of three and small, rounded flowers

Usually they chatted merrily. Today Kizzy was quiet. To make conversation, Holly said, "Those plants in the new plot still look pretty sad."

"They're not going to make it," said Kizzy.

"What's weird is that it's going to take ages to weed. Look at all that grass," said Holly.

"That's because the grass doesn't have competition from plants with wide leaves. The weed killers used on lawns kill plants with wide leaves and let the grass grow."

Holly tried to imagine having this conversation with April. She missed Kizzy when she didn't see her.

Usually Mr. Stone left the class in the garden for the first half of the period. Today, he called the class in early.

Then Mr. Stone explained the problem with the new plot. He told them his son had tested the compost they had used. It had traces of a chemical called clopyralid. He explained that clophyralid is an herbicide.

"I thought we didn't use herbicides," said one student.

"We don't," said Mr. Stone. He passed out copies of the newspaper article Kizzy had found on the Internet.

"Read this article. It will explain to you what has happened to the plants in our new plot."

When everyone had finished, they discussed the article. Mr. Stone pointed out that the source of the herbicide remained unknown. "Here is a clue though. Tell them what you figured out, Holly."

"This is the first time we have used compost from the city compost pile," said Holly.

"I have talked to Ms. Lopez," said Mr. Stone. "Tomorrow in English class she'll assign you to write letters to city council, and to the waste management department. Explain the problem. The article gives you the information. Tell them what you think they should do."

"Let's do some brainstorming now, to help you with ideas. You could think about these ideas overnight. Then you'll be prepared to write tomorrow."

"Maybe we can ask the city to tell residents not to put yard waste into the compost bins if they've used herbicides," said one boy.

"But then what will we do with the yard waste that has herbicides?" said a girl. "We don't want to send it to a landfill. Composting is good because it reduces the amount of trash we put in landfills."

"It would be better to make a law against using herbicides," said Kizzy.

"But herbicides make lawns and gardens beautiful," said April. "My parents use them to keep weeds down."

"Perhaps the environment and people's health are more important than a few weeds," said Kizzy.

April stiffened. She shot Kizzy the dirtiest look Holly had ever seen. She started whispering to Consuela, looking at Kizzy. Consuela just listened, her eyes on her desk.

Holly's head began to throb. She was proud of Kizzy. She wished she had Kizzy's courage, but she didn't. She wanted to be in the club too badly.

Mr. Stone said, "It's the state of Washington that decides which herbicides can be used and how."

After class, April and her friends waited for Kizzy in the hall. Holly walked out behind Kizzy.

"How dare you embarrass me like that? I guess people with no class don't understand the importance of a nice lawn and garden," said April, her eyes blazing.

"Not everyone agrees about what shows class," said Kizzy, her own eyes boring into April's.

"Come on, Holly," said April. "We're going to my house." She and her friends wheeled around and stalked off. Holly followed. She looked back at Kizzy, and then quickly looked away from Kizzy's accusing gaze. Her stomach squeezed into a ball.

April took them on a tour of the rose garden at her house. They walked across the lawn to a bed of roses. "See how beautiful they are?" There's not a single insect bite on them. Not a single weed in the garden." They walked to the middle of the lawn and around a circle of roses. Then they walked across the lawn to another set of roses. "These are a special breed. They attract a lot of pests. We use bug spray and weed killer and they do just fine."

As they walked across the grass again, April pointed out that nothing grew there except grass they had planted. "Now, isn't that better than a lawn full of dandelions and a garden full of weeds and bugs? If we need a few pesticides to have a beautiful lawn, so what?"

Holly saw Consuela look at the ground. Consuela lived close to Holly. Her parents didn't use pesticides in their garden. Holy wondered if Consuela felt uncomfortable too.

"May I call home?" asked Holly. "I want to tell my father where I am." Dad worked at home.

"Sure," said April.

April led them across the lawn to the kitchen door. She opened the door and they all walked in. "There's the phone," she said pointing to the wall. Holly entered her number and waited. Then she heard Skip's voice. "Hello?"

"What's up?" asked Holly.

"Just hanging out with the guys," said Skip.

"How many guys?" asked Holly. April and her friends suddenly stopped talking and started listening.

"Three of us."

"OK, I just wanted Dad to know I'm at April's."

"I figured," said Skip. "I saw Kizzy looking like someone had died. She said you left school with April and her airhead friends."

"Don't start!" said Holly. She hung up.

"Who's over?" asked April.

"Just some of Skip's friends."

"Why don't we go over to your house?" said April. All the other girls nodded and started talking at once.

Holly shrugged. "Why not?"

On the way, the girls passed Kizzy's house. Kizzy and Grace were sitting on the porch. When Kizzy saw them, she stood up, walked into the house, and closed the door. Grace turned sad eyes on Consuela for a moment. Then she followed Kizzy inside. Holly's throat tightened.

Holly opened the gate and held it. The girls walked to the front porch of Holly's house. Holly spotted a

dandelion in the lawn. She
blushed and quickly pulled it
out. April looked at the other
girls and shook her head.
Consuela blushed and kept her
eyes on the ground.

Holly opened the door for
her friends. They trooped into
the living room. Holly went
upstairs to drop her books.

"Do you have anything to
drink?" asked April.

They walked through the living room and to the
kitchen. Holly took a pitcher from the refrigerator.

"What is this?" asked April.

"Iced red clover tea with lemon," said Holly. "I can
sweeten it if you like."

"Don't you have any sodas or lemonade?" asked
April. "I don't want to drink weed tea."

"Mom doesn't buy soda. I can make some lemonade
in a few minutes," said Holly.

"OK. I'll see what the guys are doing," said April.

The door to the backyard opened off the kitchen.
April opened the door and went into the yard. She left
the door open behind her. Holly saw a yellow Frisbee sail
smoothly through the air. Jeff caught it easily.

"What are you doing, Jeff?" Holly heard April say. Through the door, she saw April smile at the boys.

"What does it look like?" said Jeff.

"Frisbee," said April. "Is it fun?"

"It was until somebody started asking stupid questions," said Jeff. Ignoring April, he tossed the Frisbee.

April turned on her heel and stomped back into the kitchen. She turned a furious gaze on Holly and said, "Your brother's friends are really rude!"

April stormed out of the kitchen and into the living room. She turned around looked fiercely at her friends. "Well, are you coming?"

The girls looked awkwardly at one another. They looked apologetically it Holly. Meekly, they followed April out the door.

Holly looked at the pitcher of lemonade she had just made. Tears squeezed out of her eyes, rolled down her cheeks, and splashed on the counter. Blinking them back, she wiped her eyes on a dish towel.

Holly picked up the pitcher of lemonade and four glasses. She carried them into the back yard. The sun hung lower, and the crisp chill was back in the air.

"Lemonade anyone?" asked Holly.

"You bet!" said Jeff.

Skip caught the Frisbee. "It's cold. Let's go in," said Skip. "Want to play monopoly, Sis?"

For the rest of the day, Holly played games with the boys. Her heart wasn't in it, but it was better than being alone.

Holly's mother came home just as the boys were leaving. She headed for the kitchen to make dinner.

"Why were your friends so rude?" asked Holly.

"They heard how April treated Kizzy. They all like Kizzy. She's been like a kid sister to us."

"April may never speak to me again."

"Maybe you should think about that," said Skip. "When April comes over, all she wants to do is hang around me and my friends. She's a pest. Haven't you noticed that she cancels on you whenever she finds out we won't be here?"

Mom overheard from the kitchen and came out to put in her two cents' worth. "That girl's a giggling flirt. Sixth grade is way too young to be chasing after boys. Especially boys in the eighth grade."

"If she was a nice birdbrain it wouldn't be so bad," said Skip. "But she's gossipy and mean. When we passed Kizzy's house, she looked like her best friend had just died. But it turned out that her best friend had just walked out on her. If you ask me, you used to be a better friend."

"I didn't ask . . ." Holly began, but she couldn't get the rest of the words past the lump in her throat. Tears oozed out again. Skip patted her shoulder. "Sorry. Let's play checkers." Holly nodded and Skip left to get the checkers.

Holly sprawled face down on the living room carpet. She started to sob. The tears splashed down and wet the carpet. Holly wiped both cheeks on the carpet. She didn't want Skip to see her crying.

Skip came in and placed a checkerboard in front of Holly. Then he plopped down on the other side.

Holly quickly dried her tears and moved first. She watched Skip carefully as he planned his first move. Skip moved, then looked up and fixed his eyes on Holly. He stared. "What's wrong with your face?"

Holly suddenly realized that her face was itchy. "Nothing," she said, "It's just itchy. How did you know?"

"Because you're getting red rashes on your cheek."

Holly stood up and looked in the mirror over the fireplace. Rashes had broken out on both her cheeks where they had touched the carpet.

Just then the doorbell rang. Skip opened the front door. Kizzy, Mr. Stone, Dr. Stone, and Kizzy's brother Mark were standing on the porch.

"I came home for one night to pick up something I need at school. I thought this would be a good time to talk about the clopyralid," said Mark.

"Come in," said Skip. Skip called Mom and Dad, and they all took seats. Kizzy sat across the room from Holly. She avoided Holly's eye.

Mark stared at Holly's face. "I've seen a rash like

that on workers who were exposed to herbicides," said Mark. "How long have you had the rash?"

"It just . . .," began Holly. She could not get any more words out. She was having trouble breathing. At first, she thought her nose was stuffed up from crying. Then she realized it was more than her nose. His chest tightened painfully. Her lungs could not pull down much air. She began to wheeze with each exhale.

Panic set in. Her heart began to pound.

"Mom! She's having an **asthma** attack," said Skip.

"That's also a reaction farm workers get from being exposed to this herbicide," said Mark. "When did this rash break out, Skip?"

"A few minutes ago."

"Where was she?"

Holly pointed, wheezing.

"Where was your face, exactly?"

Holly stood with difficulty. She had no strength in her legs. She pointed to the spot on the floor.

Dr. Stone looked at Holly's face, listened to her wheezing, and said, "She is wheezing, so she is getting some air. We'd better take her to the emergency room. It's just a precaution."

"I'd like to take a few threads of the carpet back

---

asthma – a disease of the lungs that makes it difficult to breathe

to school. I can test it for toxic substances, especially clopyralid. I can take the samples without hurting the carpet," Mark said.

"Fine! Lock up when you leave," Dad was at the door with the car keys. Mom had already picked up her purse. She brought Holly her coat. "Let's go honey," she said.

Kizzy ran up and hugged Holly. Holly was too weak to hug back. Kizzy's face fell. She dropped her arms and stepped back.

Dr. Gray was on duty at the emergency room. "Hello, Dr. Stone," he said, shaking her hand.

He examined Holly. "It does look like she was exposed to something," he said to Dr. Stone. "Her face touched it, and she probably breathed in some vapors."

"What do you think it was?" asked Mom.

"Is there something that Holly's allergic to, or was she exposed to something poisonous?"

"Can it happen from being exposed to an herbicide?" asked Mom.

"I've seen this reaction in some farm workers who went into the fields too soon after they were sprayed. Workers who spray lawns, too. This attack may have more than one cause. Were you upset, Holly?"

Holly nodded. "When you're upset, you're more likely to have an asthma attack. Exposure to a toxic substance is more likely to bring on an attack if you are also upset."

On the way home, Mom said, "After Mark tests the carpet sample, we may learn what caused the reaction. We'd better get the carpet cleaned tomorrow."

The next day, April was waiting at the door of Holly's first class. "You're not invited to my sleepover anymore," she said. Then she stepped into the classroom.

All of first period, April and her friends kept whispering and looking over at Holly.

CHAPTER 4

All Is Revealed

— OCTOBER 2001 —

Most of Holly's neighbors belonged to the Dirt Diggers Club. People from other parts of town had also joined. They met to share ideas about gardening. They often helped one another solve problems with their lawns and gardens. About half the members were organic gardeners. Some of the others avoided pesticides when they could. A few, like the Browns, used pesticides regularly.

Some people in town were growing **native plants** in their yards. These plants could resist the insect pests in the area. Therefore, insecticides were not needed.

When the club met, Will and Kizzy usually came with their parents. They hung out in Holly's room during the meeting. Tonight, Grace came too.

Holly's bedroom was upstairs, with a window that opened over the street. When Holly's door was open, she could hear the conversation from the meeting downstairs.

----

native plants – a plant found naturally in a given place

The girls felt a little weird with one another tonight. As a distraction, they opened the window. They tuned in to the conversations of club members coming up the walk. They could only hear bits.

The Browns were coming up the walk with a neighbor. "But all those dandelions and clover . . . . Don't these people take pride in their yards?" ". . . ruins the neighborhood . . . this lawn is a disgrace . . ."

"Better than ruining the creeks and rivers," said Will.

"Better than giving people cancer," said Grace. Grace's dad had cancer.

"Better than killing the fish," said Holly. "You know what, though? If people are going to gossip about each other, they should start gossiping about people who use pesticides. Mom says bugs and weeds in people's gardens should be a badge of honor."

"Why don't you suggest it to April, the queen of gossip?" asked Kizzy. Holly studied the ground.

"Shhh!" said Will. "Listen to this."

Mr. Stone was telling the Garden Club about the herbicides found in compost. He said that compost in Washington and other states had been affected. He described the problem with the school garden.

Mr. Stone told the club that Mark had tested samples from the school compost and from the town compost pile. They contained the herbicide clopyralid. He also told them about Holly's attack. Clopyralid was found in samples from the carpet. The doctor said it had probably helped bring on Holly's attack.

"That's terrible," said Grace's father. "But how did the herbicide get into the carpet?"

"Herbicides can be tracked into a home," said Dad. "Especially if somebody walks over grass that's been recently treated. Somebody walked over grass that was recently treated with clopyralid. Then they walked into our living room."

"We've known for a while that we have a problem in the water. We've been assuming it's coming from the herbicides and pesticides the farmers use. Maybe we should have been looking in our own town. People use insecticides and herbicides on lawns and gardens in town," said Mom.

"Clopyralid is illegal to use on backyards," said Mr. Stone. "It's usually only used by landscapers."

"It's perfectly legal for that," said Mr. Brown.

Mom asked, "What kind of weed killers do you use on the golf course, the park, and the city grounds?" Mr. Brown's company took care of city property.

"I don't need to discuss my business practices with you here," said Mr. Brown.

"You WILL need to discuss them with me in the city manager's office, though," said Mom.

Holly could picture Mom's eyes locked on Mr. Brown's.

The silence was so heavy Holly could feel it from upstairs. Dad changed the subject. "We've known for a while that all pesticides can have bad effects on the environment. We also know they can affect the health of people and animals. Studies show cancer rates are higher where farmers are using pesticides. They've been higher in this town than in the whole area. Maybe the solution is to start managing weeds without herbicides. The school district is already doing it. So is everybody on this block."

"Yes, and it shows!" said Mrs. Brown. "The lawns on this block are a disgrace. Nobody can have a nice lawn or garden without using weed killers and bug killers."

"Maybe clean water and wildlife are more important than your lawn and roses," said Dr. Stone.

"Maybe cancer is worse than a weedy yard with insects," said Grace's mother.

"And this herbicide may already have given one child a rash and an asthma attack," said Mom.

"That's ridiculous!" said Mrs. Brown. "I work with weed killers all the time."

"Maybe not this one," someone said.

"I think it's time to find out what's used on the golf course and city property."

The room fell silent.

"I don't think we're welcome here," said Mrs. Brown. Holly heard the front door open and slam shut.

The girls and Will looked at one another. "The weed war has begun," said Will.

For the next week, April's crowd snubbed Holly. They made nasty comments about Kizzy. "Hello Bug Lover," they would say, or "There goes the Weedy Wonder."

Holly ate lunch with Kizzy and Grace, but it wasn't like old times. Kizzy was cool to Holly, as if she didn't trust her.

The talk of the sixth grade was a big sleepover April was planning. Everyone wanted to be invited. Being invited meant you were somebody. April had carefully picked about 10 girls to invite. They included AAAs and AAA wannabees. Whenever she saw Holly nearby, April talked about the sleepover in a loud voice.

The day before the sleepover, Holly was surprised to get an email message from April.

Email

New Mail   **Reply**   **Forward**

Dear Holly,
I'm sorry I've been mean. Please come to my sleepover Friday night at 7:30.

Your friend,
April

Joy bubbled up and lifted Holly out of her seat. She practically floated to her bedroom, hugging herself. April liked her after all! Maybe she would be back in the in-crowd, or even asked to join the club.

When Holly told Mom about the party, Mom's hands went to her hips. Her eyebrows drew together. "Why do you would want to party with that crowd?"

Skip came out of his room. "You can't be serious. After the way they've treated you and Kizzy? You have too much class for them. I thought you had better values."

Holly felt tears behind her eyes. She knew Skip was right. But this was too big. It was her chance to be with the cool kids. To be respected and looked up to.

Mom looked at Holly for a long time. "It means a lot to you, doesn't it?"

Holly nodded. Skip opened his mouth. Mom threw him a warning look behind Holly's back.

Friday night, Mom drove Holly to April's. Before Holly got out of the car, Mom said, "I have a bad feeling about this party. Take my cell phone. If anything goes wrong, call me. I'll come and pick you up."

Holly thought Mom was being ridiculous. She was not about to say no to a cell phone, though.

Mrs. Brown answered the door. She seemed surprised to see Holly. "You're late. We ate dinner at 7:00," she said. Holly was sure the message said 7:30.

Mrs. Brown led Holly into the game room. A punch bowl and dessert table were set up. Ten girls were milling around and talking. Holly put her overnight bag in a bedroom off the game room.

Mrs. Brown said, "We'll go upstairs and leave you alone. Call us if you need anything."

Nobody paid any attention to Holly except to make snide comments. Holly stepped up to the dessert table. "Sorry, we don't have any weed tea," said April. Holly tried to laugh with the rest of them.

After about five minutes, everyone left the room except April and Holly. The girls came back with wrapped packages and sang "Happy Birthday" to April.

Holly wanted to disappear. Her scalp prickled with shame. She didn't know it was a birthday party.

While everyone was looking at April, Holly slipped into the bedroom where she'd left her overnight bag. She just couldn't face everyone.

Wondering what to do, she looked around the room. Her eyes fell on a picture of a baby in a heart-shaped frame. On a gold plate at the bottom, it said, "Our Valentine Baby, April Brown, born February 14, 1990."

Holly gasped. It wasn't April's birthday! April had

staged the fake birthday to make Holly feel like a loser.
Even worse, the other girls went along with it. She
cracked the door and peeked out. April had torn open an
empty package and was holding it up, laughing.

Holly grabbed her bag and slipped through a door
that opened into the back yard. She looked around for a
place to hide while she called Mom. The shed was perfect.

To take her mind off her shame, she looked around
the shed. She started reading labels on the containers.

When she came to one large can she froze. It said "active ingredient: clopyralid." She could not believe her eyes.

Holly dialed Kizzy's number on the cell phone. Kizzy answered. "It's me," said Holly.

"It must be a really dull party if you're calling me," said Kizzy.

"Don't start! I'm in the shed at April's house. I found a can of weed killer. It says 'active ingredient: clopyralid.' Isn't that the name of the weed killer they found in our compost?"

"The article said that's not legal to use in people's yards. Only licensed landscapers can use it."

"Well, it's right here. I'm looking at it."

"We need to talk about this. Mark's home for the weekend. Why don't you come over? That is, if you can tear yourself away from the party."

"Count on that!"

Holly called her mother. She waited out front.

Holly was silent on the ride home, thankful that Mom didn't ask any questions.

At home, Holly quickly changed and washed her face. She explained about the clopyralid to her parents. They all went next door.

"That's the same herbicide that turned up in all the compost piles. It's also what I found in your carpet after Holly's attack," said Mark.

"So the clopyralid is coming from their lawn clippings," said Holly.

Mr. Stone said, "They don't have enough lawn clippings to affect a large compost pile."

"I thought it was against the law for people to use it in their yards," said Kizzy.

"I think I know how the Browns got the clopyralid," said Mom. "It also explains why we have so much clopyralid in our compost. Brown Landscaping does all the gardening for the city parks. Most of the businesses use his company too. He also takes care of the grass at his golf course. That's enough lawn clippings to have a big effect on the town's compost."

"It also explains how Mrs. Brown got the clopyralid," said Mark. "Her husband gave it to her."

"I still don't know how so much clopyralid ended up on our carpet though," said Dad.

"Wait a minute!" said Skip. "Right before you had your attack April and her friends had been tromping all over the carpet. Where were they just before that?"

"At April's," said Holly.

"Did you walk on her lawn?" asked Mark.

"Yes, we walked all over it."

"Do you know when the lawn was treated with herbicide?" Mark asked.

"I'm not sure," said Holly.

"The only way to find out is to ask the Browns. We also need to talk to them about using the illegal herbicides and how they affect our town," said Mom.

"Let's all pay them a visit tomorrow," said Dr. Stone.

The next day was Saturday, Kizzy, Holly, and their parents piled into two cars and drove to April's house. Mrs. Brown was in the yard, watching a small boy run around and roll on the grass. He was about two years old.

Holly's mother was the first to get out of the car. When Mrs. Brown saw her, she said, "Come meet my grandson." She looked at him proudly.

Holly had not seen April's older brother for years. His small son looked like him.

"He's adorable," said Mom. "I wish this were a social call, but it's not."

Mrs. Brown froze. She looked around at everyone through narrowed eyes.

"The night Holly went to emergency, I took samples from the carpet where it touched her face," said Mark. "I found clopyralid. The doctor thinks it helped cause Holly's rash and asthma."

"I've already said that's ridiculous."

"The clopyralid had to be tracked in from somewhere," said Dad. "The day Holly had the attack, six girls had walked all over your lawn. Then they had walked all over the carpet at our house."

Mrs. Brown's mouth had tightened into a hard line. She glared at Dad.

"What chemicals do you use on your lawn to kill weeds?" asked Mom.

Holly had been watching the little boy. He was bending over and looking sick. Suddenly he vomited.

"Something's wrong with him!" cried Holly. She raced over to him. She looked at the puddle where he had been sick. It had chewed pieces of grass in it.

"He's been eating grass!" said Holly.

"I wasn't watching," said Mrs. Brown. "Oh! He's breaking out in a rash! But the grass shouldn't hurt him."

"That depends," said Mark. "When did you last treat it with herbicides?"

"This morning," said Mrs. Brown. "Oh, no! He's having trouble breathing!"

The boy coughed, then whimpered.

"If he can cough and cry, he's getting some air," said Dr. Stone.

"Get in the car," said Mom. "I'll drive you to the emergency room."

Mrs. Brown and her grandson crowded in with Holly's family. The Stones followed in their car.

Mrs. Brown rode in the front seat, holding her grandson. He pointed to his forehead and said "Hurt!" He whined and started to cough. He was sick again on the seat. Holly was too worried to be grossed out.

Mrs. Brown handed her cell phone to Dad. "Please call my husband. Number 2 on speed dial. Tell him to meet us at the hospital."

At the emergency room, Dr. Gray was on duty again. They told him about the boy rolling in the grass and eating it. Mrs. Brown also told him that she used clopyralid on her lawn.

"This looks as though the herbicide caused it. Young children are very sensitive to pesticides," said Dr. Gray. "He'll get over it this time. I recommend keeping him away from pesticides in the future. People exposed to herbicides and other pesticides, over time, are more likely to get serious diseases like cancer."

Mrs. Brown sank slowly into a chair. "They make the lawn and roses so beautiful," she said sadly.

The doctor picked up the boy and hugged him. "I'd say this little guy is worth more than beautiful lawns and roses."

"So would I," said Mrs. Brown.

"Me too," said a voice behind them. Mr. Brown had just arrived.

At that moment, a man walked up. His badge said he was a reporter for the town newspaper. "Any stories for me today?" he asked Dr. Gray.

"I've got one for you!" said Mr. Brown. He told the reporter he planned to stop using clopyralid on the golf course and city grounds. He pointed to Mark and said, "This young man will tell you why."

Mark told the whole story about how Holly, Kizzy, and Skip had discovered the problem with the school garden. He explained how their research led to the discovery of clopyralid in the school compost. He said two children in town had come to the emergency room with reactions to the herbicide.

Mrs. Brown admitted that her yard was the source of the clopyralid. She said she would no longer use weed killer or bug killer in her yard.

The reporter interviewed Holly, Kizzy, and Skip. He took Holly's picture. The next day, Sunday, the story and Holly's picture were on the front page. The caption described Holly's attack and that she had figured out the herbicide came from the city compost pile.

On Monday, several girls from April's sleepover apologized to Holly for making fun of her and upsetting her at the party.

April kept smiling at Holly during homeroom. During English, students asked the teacher if they could write letters to their state lawmakers. They wanted to ask them to ban the use of clopyralid in Washington State.

When Holly walked into the lunchroom, April waved for her to join the girls at her table. Holly waved and smiled. But she shook her head, and sat down with Kizzy and Grace. April's smile vanished and her face froze as she stared at Holly.

After lunch, Holly went into the girl's room. Consuela followed her in. "April was really insulted when you snubbed her at lunch. She's going to give you one more chance after school. She is going to invite you back to her house for lemonade and cookies. You'd better accept as she won't give you another chance."

"I'm going home with Kizzy," said Holly. "You can walk home with us if you like."

"Holly, I've always liked you. But I can't be nice to you if April gets mad at you. Don't you understand?"

"I understand that you're afraid of April," Holly said.

"I thought you knew how important it is to have the right friends," said Consuela. Her eyes were pleading.

"I still do," said Holly. "But now I know who the right friends are."

After school, April waited outside the classroom. "We're going to my house. Are you coming, Holly?"

"No," said Holly, "But it's nice of you to invite me. I hope you all have a good time."

April's face hardened with anger, but then relaxed into disappointment. "Okay," she said. "See you around."

EPILOGUE

Roses Without Poison

— SEPTEMBER 2002 —

The Browns' rose garden was in full bloom. About a hundred people milled around the yard. The party was to showcase how beautiful Mrs. Brown had made the garden without pesticides.

The town had been shocked by the article about the herbicide sending children to the hospital. When people read about the problems with the compost, they declared war on clopyralid. Dr. Grey wrote an article for the local newspaper. He explained that all pesticides could cause health problems in people and animals. Some of the problems did not occur for many years.

More and more, people found ways to manage without pesticides in their homes and gardens. Some began using more native plants in their yards.

A year ago, Brown Landscaping had stopped using pesticides. A few fish began to turn up in the creek. Washington State had also banned clopyralid.

The AAAs were in one corner of the yard with Holly, Kizzy, and Grace. Everyone was cracking up at Kizzy's jokes. They didn't all hang out together. They all got along in large groups, though.

Holly, Kizzy, Grace, and Consuela had made the soccer team. They all walked home from practice together. They were happy with their own little group.

Jeff's sister Linda was captain of the soccer team. In seventh grade Linda and her friends were more popular than the AAAs, and they were not mean. Holly was happy with her neighborhood crowd though.

Holly looked around the party. It was nice to see everyone getting along. Even better, it was nice to know that no poisons lurked in this beautiful garden. Best of all, she was going fishing tomorrow. Jeff and his sister were coming. This time they may catch some fish.

Why People Use Pesticides

Pesticides can help make lawns look nice with less work. They also have many other uses. These chemicals allow farmers to grow food with less work. Many farmers treat their fields with pesticides. This keeps bugs and weeds from damaging crops. Grocery store customers often want perfect-looking produce. Pesticides help farmers grow produce that looks perfect.

Pesticides also help control diseases. Illnesses like malaria are carried by insects. Pesticides can kill the mosquitoes that carry malaria. This saves lives.

Banning Clopyralid

Clopyralid is a real pesticide. And it created a real problem. People in Washington State began to notice something suspicious. Some of their flowers and vegetables were dying off in gardens. The gardeners had used compost from city supplies. The compost should have helped the plants grow, but it was poisoning them.

How could Washington State protect its compost? The answer was a ban on clopyralid in 2002. People couldn't use it on lawns. Golf courses could use it only if grass clippings from the course didn't go to a city composting site. The ban has paid off. Clopyralid in compost dropped by 80 percent in 2003. It dropped another 9 percent in 2004.

What Is Organic?

You may have seen foods labeled "organic" in the grocery store. By law, these foods are grown using natural methods. No chemicals can be used except those that occur in nature. Organic farming keeps dangerous pesticides out of the food supply. It also reduces the amount of pesticide being carried by water from fields into rivers and streams.

Organic farmers also only use natural fertilizers. This keeps poisonous fertilizers out of the land and water.

Write a Newspaper Column

Many people still use pesticides. Like the Browns, they like the benefits and don't realize the dangers. Write an essay for your school newspaper. List the pros and cons of pesticides. Tell your classmates about safer options for growing healthy plants.

- What are the benefits of pesticides?

- What harm can they cause?

- Are pesticides necessary?

- Is there any time when a pesticide is the best option?

Now write down questions of your own. Put answers next to your questions as you find them. Write your essay based on your research.

Read More About Growing Food

Find and read more books about growing food. As you read, think about these questions. They will help you understand more about the topic.

- How is food grown?
- Why do farmers use pesticides and herbicides?
- What decisions do farmers have to make?
- How does farming affect the environment?

SUGGESTED READING
Reading Expeditions
Science Issues Today:
Feeding the World